THE LIBRARY OF CONTEMPORARY THOUGHT

*America's most original voices
tackle today's most provocative issues*

JOHN FEINSTEIN

THE FIRST COMING
Tiger Woods: Master or Martyr?

"Now twenty-two, he is indescribably wealthy—his endorsement deals with Nike, Titleist, and American Express alone are worth close to $100 million—and there is no material item on the planet that he can't have. What's more, he is making all this money playing a game he loves; living out a dream that has been part of his life for as long as he can remember.

"Therein lies the problem. If there is one thing in his life that Tiger cannot own outright, it is his dream. He has to share that. He shares it with a father who honestly believes that *he* is responsible for Tiger's greatness. He shares it with a management company that sees him as a money machine that must be pumped dry before he escapes. He shares it with corporate sponsors who expect time, charm, and victories in return for their millions. And he shares it with a public that wants him to be the sweet, sensitive guy it sees in his commercials and is shocked and dismayed when he turns out to be a twenty-two-year-old who tells dirty jokes, stamps his foot when he doesn't get his way, and stalks angrily off golf courses when '

D1019919

THE FIRST COMING

Tiger Woods:
Master or Martyr

JOHN FEINSTEIN

THE LIBRARY OF CONTEMPORARY THOUGHT
THE BALLANTINE PUBLISHING GROUP • NEW YORK

The Library of Contemporary Thought
Published by The Ballantine Publishing Group

Copyright © 1998 by John Feinstein

All rights reserved under International and Pan-American Copyright Conventions. Published in the United States by The Ballantine Publishing Group, a division of Random House, Inc., New York, and simultaneously in Canada by Random House of Canada Limited, Toronto.

http://www.randomhouse.com

Library of Congress Cataloging-in-Publication Data
Feinstein, John.
  The first coming : Tiger Woods, master or martyr / John Feinstein.—1st ed.
      p.   cm.
  ISBN 0-345-42286-4 (alk. paper)
  1. Woods, Tiger. 2. Golfers—United States—Biography.
I. Title.
GV964.W66F45   1998
796.352'092—dc21
[B]   97-52660
                                                   CIP

Text design by Holly Johnson
Cover design by Ruth Ross
Cover photo © J.D. Cuban/Allsport

Manufactured in the United States of America

First Edition: March 1998

10   9   8   7   6   5   4   3   2   1

D AY ONE OF the 1997 United States Open.
At exactly noon, Tiger Woods, once known
as Eldrick, now known as golf's messiah, stepped
onto the first tee at the Congressional Country
Club with playing partners Steve Jones and Tom
Lehman. Jones was the defending Open champion.
Lehman was the reigning British Open champion. Among the thousands pressed against the
gallery ropes, five and six deep from tee to green,
there might have been a hundred who were there
to see the two Open titleholders.

Everyone else had come to see Tiger. He was
twenty-one years old, a multi-*multi*-millionaire, and

already a one-name athlete, as in Michael or Shaq, Deion or The Shark. Only, at that moment Tiger was bigger than all of them. Even Michael. He was nine weeks removed from one of the most stunning performances in the history of sports, a twelve-shot victory in the Masters that had left people in golf groping for words to describe what they had seen. And what they had seen was impossible. "He's a boy among men," Tom Watson had said at the time. "And he's teaching the men a lesson."

The Masters had elevated Woods to a level of fame that perhaps no athlete other than Muhammad Ali had ever achieved. People who knew absolutely nothing about golf, cared not at all about the sport, stopped to watch Tiger play. Children who once wanted to "be like Mike" and slam-dunk from the free-throw line now wanted to be Tiger and hit 350-yard drives. He signed endorsement contracts for staggering amounts of money. He blew off the president of the United States and Rachel Robinson, the widow of the century's most important athlete—and made no apologies for it. He didn't have to. He was Tiger. They weren't.

His arrival on the grounds of Congressional at the start of the week had made a presidential motorcade look understated. Every time he moved, thousands moved with him. He was surrounded by so many security people that even other *players* were hesitant to approach him for fear they might get knocked backward by a large, unsmiling man in sunglasses. Miraculously, Woods seemed perfectly at ease with it all. At one point, lingering on the driving range while dozens of media types stood at a respectful distance, Woods looked at a couple of friends and said, "Watch this."

He took five steps to his left, as if to leave the range. The security force immediately began to form a wedge, advance men flying toward the ropes to clear the area lest some fan momentarily impede Tiger's exit. The media also began moving. Cameras were hoisted onto shoulders, tape recorders began whirring, notebooks were scribbled in. Then Tiger stopped. The wedge stopped instantly. The media, of course, also stopped. Tiger smiled, turned, and walked back to where he had been standing. It was a remarkable display of absolute power.

Now, three days later, Woods stood on the first

tee, appearing cool, calm, and collected. After Ron Read, the United States Golf Association's (USGA) official starter, had introduced him, Woods gave the cheering throngs his now-trademark thousand-watt smile and set up over his ball. His club came back in the long, graceful arc that even his fellow pros envy, and then it came down, whipping through the hitting area with such force that the nearby grandstand seemed likely to start shaking. The ball climbed into the sky, becoming a tiny dot against the fluffy clouds overhead; it hung there while all the spectators gaped, and then it came down 290 yards away—it was just a 3-wood—on the right side of the fairway. As soon as it rolled to a stop on the short grass, the gallery exploded in appreciation. Woods reached down, plucked up his tee, and began marching down the fairway. He was the eye of the hurricane, cameramen and photographers scrambling to record his every step, fans cheering and applauding and calling his name as he, Lehman, and Jones moved toward their tee shots. If Lehman or Jones had keeled over in the middle of the fairway, it's possible that no one would have noticed.

When it was his turn to hit, Woods looked carefully at the green, now less than 150 yards away, consulted at length with his caddy, Mike "Fluff" Cowan (who had become a huge celebrity himself, thanks to his boss's success), and then took a long time before selecting a wedge for his second shot. It is an understatement to call Woods deliberate. All around America, young golfers are now learning to play the game ve-e-ry slo-o-wly because they are mimicking Woods. Finally he set up over his ball, took the club back in the same gorgeous arc, and gently lofted the ball in the direction of the green. When it came down, it hit and spun to a halt no more than six feet from the pin. The crowd exploded yet again. Woods smiled once more as Fluff handed him his putter.

In the press tent, Gary Van Sickle of *Sports Illustrated* shrugged. "That's it," he said. "It's over. Put his name on the trophy."

Van Sickle was joking. Well, half joking. But he wasn't the only person on the grounds thinking that way. When it was Woods's turn to attempt his birdie putt a few minutes later, he surveyed the putt from every possible angle. When he got over the ball, he took one, two, three practice putts. Marriages have started, ended, and restarted in the time it takes Woods to line up a putt. Finally he pulled the trigger. The crowd prepared to roar again. But somehow the ball squirted right. Woods stared at it for a moment, as if it must have gone out-of-round to stay out of the hole.

All around him there were shouts of encouragement. "No problem, Tiger," someone yelled. "Seventeen under will do." Woods tapped in for par. No big deal. After all, he had shot 40 on the first nine holes at the Masters and won by twelve. One missed birdie putt was not a problem.

Not for Tiger Woods.

ALMOST FIVE HOURS later Woods, Lehman, and Jones stood on the eighteenth tee. All were tired. It had been a hot, humid afternoon, and Congressional is a golf course that beats players down even under the best conditions. Lehman was the most satisfied of the three, since he was three under par, just two shots behind the leader, Colin Montgomerie. Jones had scrambled all day and was a respectable two over par. He wasn't happy, but he wasn't unhappy, either.

Woods was fuming. Through ten holes, he had been two under par. But then he had found trouble. Congressional was not Augusta, the home of the Masters. The fairways weren't wide open. The rough was high. Mistakes were costly. Woods had played the last seven holes in four over par. Like Jones, he was two over for the day. Hardly disastrous, but aggravating. The eighteenth at Congressional is a 190-yard par 3 with water in front of the green and to the left. It is not a difficult hole, but it can be a troublesome one if a player is too bold. Tiger Woods is nothing if not bold. At times he goes beyond bold to reckless.

Clearly, the smart thing to do at this juncture in the day was to play to the center of the green. Lehman and Jones did just that, lofting their iron shots safely to the right of the pin, away from the water. Woods wasn't thinking about safety. He was thinking about getting close, making a birdie, and giving himself some momentum for the second round. There is no shot in golf that Woods doesn't think he can pull off. That is part of his greatness. And so he pulled a 5-iron, aimed directly at the flag tucked on the left side of the green near the water, and let fly.

The ball was too far left the minute it came off the club. Woods stared in disbelief. His lips formed the word *down*, indicating he wanted the ball to get down on dry ground as quickly as possible. The ball wasn't listening. It bounced on the slope to the left of the green, took one bounce, and splashed into the water. There was a groan from the thousands around the green, then shocked silence.

In golf, they call that day's pin placement at the eighteenth hole a sucker pin. The idea is that only a sucker would try to get close to such a pin. In full view of millions of TV viewers, the messiah had turned into a sucker, and he did not take to the new role well. Tiger played his third shot from the drop area onto the green and two-putted for a double-bogey 5. That gave him 74 for the day. The thousand-watt smile was nowhere to be found when he finally holed out.

Craig Smith, who handles the media for the USGA, had been prepared for the possibility that Woods would play poorly. He knew that if Tiger played well, there would be no problem asking him to hop on a golf cart and ride down to the massive media tent that had been set up for the Open adjacent to Congressional's outdoor tennis courts. But Smith also knew that on those rare

occasions in the past when a golf course had refused to roll over and play dead for Woods, he had
been less than cooperative with the media. Three
weeks earlier, at the Colonial Invitational in Fort
Worth, Texas, Woods had led the tournament during the final round, only to fade to fourth place at
the end. He had refused to come to the interview
room after the round, and when a few reporters
had had the audacity to walk into the locker room
to try to talk to him, they had been ordered to
leave by Woods's security people. That week the
PGA Tour sent a note to Team Tiger: In the future,
his security people were to stay outside the locker
room. And the Tour—not Woods—would decide
who was welcome in there and who was not.

Smith couldn't have the world's most famous
golfer blowing off the media after the first round
of the U.S. Open, whether he shot 64 or 74 or 84.
So he had taken steps to make it as easy as possible
for Woods in case he didn't play well. Instead of
going to the media tent, Woods would simply have
to veer to his right as he walked up the hill from
the scorer's tent to the locker room. There, Smith
had told the media to set up on the back balcony

of the clubhouse. Woods could walk to a podium, answer a few questions, then go directly to the locker room. Smith wanted to make it as painless as possible for an agitated Tiger.

Only, that wasn't good enough. As soon as Woods walked out of the tent he informed Smith's people he wouldn't be talking to the media that day. They tried to explain the setup, pointing to the balcony. Woods shook his head and kept walking. Smith knew that an explanation such as "Tiger has declined to speak" wasn't going to be good enough on this day at this tournament. Most golfers understand that part of their job is to talk to the media after they play, regardless of their score. Already that day Greg Norman, Fred Couples, Davis Love III, and Phil Mickelson, all of whom had finished with scores higher than Tiger's, had patiently answered questions about their aggravating trips around Congressional.

Woods wasn't as old as any of them, nor was he as mature. He also hadn't had to deal with failure very often, and even though a 74 didn't, by any means, knock him out of contention to win the tournament, at that moment it felt like a giant catastrophe. Craig Smith understood that. He also understood that Woods was going to have many other days like this in his golf career and he might as well get used to the fact that talking to the media on those days was as much a part of the deal as the millions all those corporations were throwing at his feet.

So Smith followed Woods into the locker room and patiently explained to him that all he needed to do was take a few minutes to answer some basic questions and then he could bolt. But Woods was already bolting—he stormed out of the locker room, up the steps, and out the back door of the clubhouse to where his courtesy car was parked. Melanie Hauser, who had been assigned by the Golf Writers Association of America to play pool reporter in case of another Tiger bolt, was right behind him.

"Tiger," she said, "if you don't talk to me, you're going to get ripped, I mean really ripped."

Woods kept walking. "Tiger," Hauser continued as Woods reached his car, "take two minutes."

Woods had the car door open now. He had thrown his audio headset into the backseat so hard that Hauser was convinced he had broken it. "Okay," he said finally. "What?"

Hauser did the best she could, asking Woods to review the round. What had gone wrong on the back nine? Did he need to make adjustments for the next day? Could he still win? Woods's longest answer was seven words. When he had answered the last question, he got in the car, slammed the door, and drove off. He looked very much like what he was: an angry twenty-one-year-old kid who hadn't gotten his way.

But he was also the messiah. And his disciples were waiting to tell him that he was still perfect. Which was the last thing Tiger Woods needed to hear that day.

THAT JUNE DAY—and its aftermath—provides a textbook example of why it is so difficult to be Eldrick "Tiger" Woods. Not that his life is a difficult one to live most days. Now twenty-two, he is indescribably wealthy—his endorsement deals with Nike, Titleist, and American Express alone are worth close to $100 million—and there is no material item on the planet that he can't have. What's more, he is making all this money playing a game he loves, living out a dream that has been a part of his life for as long as he can remember.

Therein lies the problem. If there is one thing

in his life that Tiger cannot own outright, it is his dream. He has to share that. He shares it with a father who honestly believes that *he* is responsible for Tiger's greatness. He shares it with a management company that sees him as a money machine that must be pumped dry before he escapes. He shares it with corporate sponsors who expect time, charm, and victories in return for their millions. And he shares it with a public that wants him to be the sweet, sensitive guy it sees in his commercials and is shocked and dismayed when he turns out to be a twenty-two-year-old who tells dirty jokes, stamps his foot when he doesn't get his way, and stalks angrily off golf courses when he shoots 74.

It has been said in the past that when an athlete puts a corporate logo on his body or his equipment, he sells off a piece of his soul. If that is the case, Tiger Woods has very little soul left to work with, because almost everything he owns—from cap to shoes, golf bag to golf balls, even his free time—has been sold. In the corporate world the term is "golden handcuffs." Even when he is on the golf course, playing the game he loves to play,

Woods isn't completely free. He is always under the microscope. No matter how he plays, the public wants an explanation.

When he stormed off after that opening 74 at Congressional in June 1997, leaving Melanie Hauser with a couple of meaningless sound bites, Woods knew he was wrong. He knew because he's a bright young man who comprehends the difference between right and wrong. He knew because he understands the traditions of golf and respects them. He knew because a few months earlier when he had complained to Arnold Palmer that the public and the media wouldn't let him be a normal twenty-one-year-old, Palmer had looked him in the eye and said, "Tiger, normal twenty-one-year-olds don't have fifty million dollars in the bank."

But when he drove away from the golf course, he also knew that there were people waiting to tell him he *hadn't* done anything wrong. His chief apologist is a man named Hughes Norton, who works for the International Management Group. IMG is the most powerful and omnipresent sports management company in the world. In fact, it isn't limited to sports: At one time the pope was an IMG client. Seriously.

To Hughes Norton, the Woods family is far more important than the pope or anyone else he has ever represented, a list that once included people such as Greg Norman and Curtis Strange. (In recent years Norman has left IMG and Strange has asked for a different agent.) Norton lost his position as director of IMG's golf division but remained a powerful figure inside the company because he began recruiting Earl Woods when Woods's son was just a teenager. Norton took no chances on losing the prodigy that Earl and his wife, Kutilda, had produced. At one point he put Earl Woods, who had retired to live on a military pension in 1988, on the IMG payroll, listing him as a "junior talent scout." There was no doubting the fact that, when the time came, Earl was going to deliver at least one junior with loads of talent.

As long as the Woods family is happy with IMG, IMG is happy with Hughes Norton. No one understands that better than Norton, who, with degrees from Yale and Harvard, is nobody's fool. A youthful-looking fifty, Norton is one of those agents who can charm and intimidate in the same sentence. He first joined IMG in 1972 and conducts himself with the kind of arrogance—"we're IMG and you're not"—that seems ingrained in many of the company's employees. But now Norton's future with the company is very much intermingled with the Woods family.

That's why Norton has defended every move Tiger has made since the afternoon of August 27, 1996, when, with Earl sitting a few feet away on the podium and Norton and Kutilda sitting together in the audience, Tiger stepped to a microphone in Milwaukee, Wisconsin, and smoothly delivered the scripted line "Hello, world." Everyone in the room laughed at the opening. How clever, they all thought. They were right. The line was so clever that it had already been filmed as part of a Nike commercial that hit the air forty-eight hours later. Not that the decision to turn pro, sign with IMG, and make a $43 million deal with Nike had been preplanned. Of course not. And Santa knows who's been naughty and who's been nice. It had, if you believed Team Tiger, all just come together in the forty-eight hours after Woods dramatically won a third straight U.S. Amateur title, coming from five holes down to beat a sophomore from the University of Florida named Steve Scott on the second hole of sudden death. When his winning putt dropped, Tiger Woods didn't go to console or congratulate Steve Scott, he went to hug Earl Woods. Cameras were rolling. First things first.

And so when Woods stormed away from Congressional ten months after that hug and less than ten weeks after becoming the Masters champion, Norton and friends were waiting for him—not to explain to him that being Tiger Woods meant dealing with certain responsibilities after bad rounds as well as good ones, but to tell him how unfair it all was that he had to put up with so many demands.

The next morning Woods showed what kind of competitor he is, putting the 74 in his rearview mirror with a superb 67. That put him right back into contention, jumping him from nine shots back of the leader to four shots back, in a tie for seventh place. This time Tiger was happy to come to the media tent to meet with all the cameras, tape recorders, and notebooks. Several minutes into the press conference, someone asked him about his postround performance the day before. Woods was prepped and ready.

"The thing is, I think that's a double standard," he said. "Do you require, I guess, Greg Norman or Steve Elkington or Phil Mickelson who ended up at five over to come in? They don't require that. And for me, I have to come in. And I just want to be considered one of a hundred and fifty-six players playing the tournament. And if I'm not near the lead, then I shouldn't be required to answer questions."

The answer was both disingenuous and inaccurate. All the players Woods mentioned *had* spoken to the media after their rounds. They hadn't come to the media tent, but no one had asked Woods to do that either, and he knew it. As for wanting to be considered just one of 156 players, he knew full well how ludicrous that comment was. Tiger Woods has never—*ever*—been just one of the players. He doesn't *want* to be just one of the players, except when it suits his purposes. He wants to be one of one, *the* one and only. That is the trait that has made him great. For him to hide behind the I'm-just-another-player excuse was both silly and intellectually dishonest. And no one in the room knew that better than he did.

Often when athletes make excuses for inexcusable behavior, the media swallow them. Woods had already been let off easy for a number of other off-course mistakes and indiscretions, in part because of his youth, in part because of his stardom. But on that day at Congressional the media had heard enough. Or too much. Even those among them who had become informal members of Team Tiger admitted that the time had come for someone to sit down and talk to him. One IMG operative even conceded there was concern about Tiger's apparent lack of respect for almost everyone. "The problem," he said, "is that he's starting to believe all that messiah stuff."

Which leads us back to the beginning of our story.

N O SPORT HAS needed a black superstar more than golf. That's because no sport has had more of a racist image than golf. It wasn't until November 1961—almost a year into John F. Kennedy's administration—that the PGA of America removed the Caucasians-only clause from its constitution. That move was inspired not by the desire to do what was right but by a threat from California attorney general Stanley Mosk to ban the Tour from the state on the grounds of discrimination and to further recommend to other state attorneys general that they do the same.

During the next decade, a number of black

players enjoyed successful careers on tour, among them Charlie Sifford and Pete Brown, who both won tournaments. Back then, a victory on tour did not mean a player was automatically invited to play in the Masters at the lily-white Augusta National Golf Club. Not surprisingly, neither Sifford nor Brown was asked to play at Augusta. It was not until 1975, when the rules had been changed to afford any tournament winner an automatic invitation to the event, that Lee Elder became the first African-American inside Augusta's ropes who wasn't carrying someone else's golf bag.

Fifteen years later, when the PGA Championship was scheduled to be played at Shoal Creek Country Club in Birmingham, Alabama, Hall Thompson, the club's founder and owner, was asked by a local reporter what would happen if a black were to apply for membership in his club. "That just wouldn't happen in Birmingham," Thompson replied.

The comment set off a firestorm that almost led to the tournament's being scheduled at a different venue. Beyond that, it raised questions about professional golf tournaments being played at all-white clubs. By the end of the year, the PGA Tour, the PGA of America, and the USGA had all passed rules requiring that any private club hosting one of their events had to have minority membership. Most clubs—but not all—complied and quickly scrambled to find at least one minority member. Augusta National, though technically not associated with any of the three groups, also invited its first African-American to join.

Shoal Creek became a symbol of golf's inaccessibility to minorities. This wasn't exactly new, but the incident focused attention on it all over again. Baseball, football, and basketball were all minority-dominated by the 1990s. Even tennis had Althea Gibson in the 1950s and Arthur Ashe in the 1960s and 1970s. When Gibson won Wimbledon and the U.S. Open in 1957 and 1958, the PGA's Caucasians-only clause still existed. Now, nearly forty years later, people began to notice that there were virtually no blacks on the PGA Tour. The best black golfers—Sifford, Brown, Elder, Calvin Peete, Jim Dent, Ted Rhodes—were retired or on the senior tour. The caddy programs that had produced them were virtually dead, replaced by golf carts.

The only African-American member of the PGA Tour in the mid-1990s was Jim Thorpe, a three-time winner on tour. But Thorpe hadn't won since 1986 and was struggling to retain his exempt status until he turned fifty in 1999 and could join the senior tour.

"We have a very serious problem," Tim Finchem said, shortly after becoming commissioner of the PGA Tour in 1994. "Our tour looks nothing like our country looks."

And then along came Tiger Woods.

Golf people first began hearing his name in the late 1980s, when he began tearing up junior tournaments in California. He was a skinny kid with a whiplike swing who drove the ball amazing distances and, so the legend went, had been trained since birth by his father, a former Green Beret, to become golf's first black superstar.

Of course, Earl Woods wasn't very different from other pushy parents who look at their sons and daughters and see dollar signs and celebrity status. The term "Little League parent" has now been extended to include tennis parents, skating parents, gymnastics parents, and, more recently, golf parents. What made Earl Woods different from most of those parents was that he was one of the lucky ones: His kid had talent. Huge talent.

No matter how many books Earl Woods writes about teaching Tiger to be tough by screaming and yelling at him and throwing things at him on the driving range, none of it would have mattered if the son hadn't been blessed with extraordinary physical gifts. The fact that Tiger (whose nickname comes from a Vietnamese officer Earl Woods fought with in Vietnam) is bright and competitive certainly helps. But there are a lot of bright, tough, competitive people in the world with handicaps of twelve.

Tiger appeared on TV on the *Mike Douglas Show* at the age of two; he allegedly shot 48 for nine holes at age three, and he was first mentioned in *Golf Digest* when he was five. At fifteen he won the U.S. Junior Amateur championship, then won it again the next two years. No one in history had ever won it more than once. At eighteen he became the youngest player to win the U.S. Amateur, then won the Amateur again in 1995 and in 1996,

becoming the first player ever to win three con-
secutive Amateurs.

After he won the Amateur for the first time in
1994, there were rumors he would pass up his
scholarship to Stanford and go directly to the pros.
He didn't—but throughout his two years in college, rumors that he would turn pro any minute
were rampant. By the time he won the third Amateur title, no one alive thought he was going to be
spending the fall as a Stanford junior. Phil Knight,
the CEO of Nike, wasn't traipsing around after
Woods during his matches at Pumpkin Ridge Golf
Club, outside of Portland, Oregon, because he
had suddenly been overwhelmed by a love for
amateur golf.

Everyone on the PGA Tour had been waiting
for Woods. They knew the game desperately
needed a black star; they knew it was only a matter
of time until Woods became the Tour's first black
superstar; and they also knew that his success could
only help them. Higher TV ratings, higher atten-
dance, more corporate interest—all that would
add up to more money for everyone. But no

one—absolutely no one—had any idea what his impact on the game would be. The arrival of Tiger Woods on the PGA Tour changed the sport more than the arrival of any athlete in any game since Jackie Robinson.

"Hello, world," Woods said in that first Nike commercial. "Are you ready for me?"

In many ways, the answer was no.

IT WASN'T AS if Woods was the first young star to
arrive in the professional sports world with a lot
of hype. The most recent example of a young athlete being billed as a savior—before his or her first
official appearance as a representative of corporate
America—is the sad story of Jennifer Capriati. In
1990, at the age of thirteen, she burst upon the
tennis world billed as the next Chris Evert. Tennis
desperately needed another Evert, since the original had retired at the end of 1989. Along came
Capriati, who was pretty, hailed from Florida also,
and had a ludicrous amount of game for someone
so young. By the time she hit her first serve as a

professional she had corporate contracts worth millions and her father and her management company were marketing her worldwide as the future of women's tennis. Her management company? Why, IMG, of course. Her father planned to write a book about how he had shaped and molded young Jennifer into a champion.

But Stefano Capriati wasn't quite as fortunate as Earl Woods. His I-me-my-mine book never got written, because Jennifer was out of tennis long before her eighteenth birthday.

It wasn't so much playing Wimbledon and the French Open at fourteen that drove Capriati from the game. Rather, it was the demands made by her father and IMG in the name of raking in money. When she returned from her first European trip— eight weeks overseas—she wasn't home for a week before she was dragged off to New Hampshire to play in a meaningless exhibition so she could cash in on a $150,000 guarantee. At the end of that first year, when she was exhausted from all the playing and traveling and smiling and talking, she was sent off to Japan, in part to pick up another guarantee, in part to keep the corporate sponsors happy.

One scene sums up what happened to Jennifer Capriati. In 1991, a year after she had come to Paris as the golden girl, she was upset in the fourth round of the French Open on an outside court. Devastated, Capriati gathered her things and began walking off the court. Her eyes searched the corner of the stands where she knew her parents had been sitting during the match. Clearly, she needed a look of encouragement or someone nodding at her to tell her it was okay. But Stefano and Denise Capriati were nowhere in sight. As soon as the match had ended, Stefano Capriati had stormed out of the grandstand, his wife right behind him, so he could yell at the people from IMG for allowing his daughter to be scheduled to play on an outside court.

Two years later, in September of 1993, Capriati lost a first-round match at the U.S. Open, left the court in tears, and walked away from tennis. She ended up being arrested once for shoplifting and then for drug possession. She became the symbol of how out-of-control adults can ruin the career—not to mention the life—of a talented child.

Both Earl and Tiger Woods bridle angrily

when comparisons are made between them and the Capriatis. Tiger was twenty when he turned pro, not thirteen, and he had two years of college behind him. What's more, his first year on the Tour would indicate that he's going to be around a lot longer and have a lot more success than Jennifer Capriati, now slogging along trying to make a comeback at the ancient (for tennis) age of twenty-two.

But the comparisons are legitimate. Both fathers willingly turned their children into meal tickets long before they had turned pro. Stefano Capriati stopped working when his daughter was nine to "coach" her. The only job Earl Woods has held since 1988 was the one provided for him by Hughes Norton and IMG. Both were willing to take credit early and often for the success of their children. There *is* a difference, though: brainpower. No one would ever mistake either Capriati for a rocket scientist. Jennifer Capriati is a sweet girl who simply couldn't handle the pressures brought to bear on her. Tiger Woods may chafe under those pressures, may make mistakes—*has* made mistakes—but, in the end, he can handle it because he's smart, tough, and shrewd. He is exactly three months older than Jennifer Capriati but is light-years ahead when it comes to maturity and street smarts.

When Capriati began to lose matches and face some criticism, it destroyed her self-confidence and made her miserable. Woods clearly doesn't enjoy being criticized (who does?), but he can deal with it. After he won the Masters, there were people willing to hand golf's Grand Slam to him as if it were a given. Deep down, he may have thought those people were right. After all, winning the Masters was *easy*. But golf never stays easy for long, no matter who you are, no matter how blessed you may be. Woods didn't seriously challenge in any of 1997's remaining three majors; his highest finish was nineteenth place at the U.S. Open. Then he bombed out at the Ryder Cup, going 1-3-1, including an embarrassing loss in the singles to Costantino Rocca.

All that meant was that he still had a lot of learning to do. In all, his first full year on tour was an amazing one—four victories, a new record for prize money, and the runaway Masters. He was a dominant player in a sport that is almost impossible to dominate. But as limitless as his future appears to be, there are still potential pitfalls. Not with his golf game, which no doubt will get better with each passing year. The question remains: Is there anyone out there willing to tell Tiger Woods that he's *not* the messiah?

THE WHOLE MESSIAH thing began in December 1996 when *Sports Illustrated* inexplicably decided to make Woods its Sportsman of the Year. Mike Lupica, the *New York Daily News*'s superb columnist, summed up that decision better than anyone when he said, "It's the first time they've given someone Sportsman of the Year based on spec."

Which was exactly right. What Woods did in 1996 was extraordinary—for a twenty-one-year-old. He won the U.S. Amateur title and then, in just eight pro tournaments, he won twice, finished in the top five three other times, and brought home a staggering $790,594. He did all this with the whole world—not just the whole golf world—watching. But Sportsman of the Year? He wasn't even the golfer of the year, unless you factor in his age and inexperience, which *SI* isn't supposed to do. If age is a factor, then George Bush should be the 1997 Sportsman of the Year for jumping out of an airplane at the age of seventy-two.

Sports Illustrated sent Gary Smith, its best writer, to write the Sportsman of the Year story on Woods. In talking to Earl Woods, Smith got quotes in which the father insisted that his son had been sent by God and that he would be the most important human ever—not the most important golfer or the most important athlete, but the most important *human*. "Tiger will do more than any other man in history to change the course of humanity," Earl Woods said. When Smith asked Earl Woods if he honestly thought his son—a golfer— would have more impact than Nelson Mandela, more than Gandhi, more than the Buddha, Earl Woods didn't blink. "Yes, because he has a larger forum than any of them. Because he's playing a sport that's international. Because he's qualified through his ethnicity to accomplish miracles. He's the bridge between the East and the West. There is no limit because he has the guidance. I don't know yet exactly what form this will take, but he is the Chosen One. He'll have the power to impact nations. Not people. *Nations.* The world is just getting a taste of his power." Earl Woods also explained that he had been personally selected by God to nurture this more-than-mere-mortal creature.

Rather than take those words and bury Earl Woods with them, Smith ended up praising him. By the end of the piece, Smith came up just short of describing Tiger's birth in a manger.

The timing of the story and Earl's comments were not precipitous. Tiger had already become something of an outcast in his new environment, in part because of simple, outright jealousy, but also because of the way he and his handlers had conducted themselves during his victory lap through the 1996 fall swing of the Tour.

It started at the Greater Milwaukee Open in Tiger's debut week, when several players overheard Earl demanding twenty-five comp tickets, pointing out to tournament officials that Tiger's presence had probably doubled their ticket sales. That may have been true, but none of the other players really wanted to hear Earl yelling about it.

That was a relatively minor problem. Tiger finished sixtieth that week, making $2,544 in his pro debut. His goal was to make about $170,000 in the eight tournaments left in the year in order to finish in the top 125 on the money list for the season so he could avoid a trip to the Tour's dreaded qualifying school. If he made the top 125, he would be an exempt player for 1997, meaning he could play wherever and whenever he wanted. If he didn't make the top 125, he would have to be one of the 40 low finishers in a field of 190 who played six rounds the first week in December for the chance to play on tour the next year.

A lot of players wondered if Tiger could make the $170,000 in eight weeks. The last player who had earned a spot on tour that way had been Justin Leonard in 1994. But Leonard had turned pro in July and had played in thirteen events, just squeezing into one of the final exempt spots. Woods quieted the doubters quickly. After Milwaukee he finished eleventh in Canada, fifth at the Quad City

Classic (after leading through three rounds), and tied for third at the B.C. Open. Those finishes gave him $140,000 in earnings with four weeks left to go. By the time he arrived at the Buick Challenge in Callaway Gardens, Georgia, for his fifth event, he was a virtual lock to gain an exemption. He was also very tired. Although the plan had been for him to play eight straight weeks in order to earn his money, he was already finding life on tour a grind, especially since he had to deal with so much away from the golf course—interviews, photo shoots, time to consult with Team Tiger, commercial shoots—each and every day.

Woods had been able to play in all of these events because he had been granted sponsor's exemptions. Each tournament director is given four sponsor's exemptions, which can be used any way the director wishes. Most of the time they are given to local pros, old-timers from the area who are no longer exempt, an up-and-coming amateur, or, in this case, a rising star who isn't yet an exempt player on tour. When Justin Leonard turned pro in 1994 he received a number of sponsor's exemptions by writing letters to the tournament directors, requesting them. Tiger Woods never had to write any letters.

In fact, he had been granted a sponsor's exemption to the Buick Challenge even before he turned pro. Since Stanford doesn't start classes until October, Woods had planned in the spring to play several Tour events in September, regardless of whether or not he turned pro. When the people who run the annual Fred Haskins Dinner, which honors the collegiate golfer of the year, found out that Woods would be playing in the Buick Challenge, they arranged to hold their dinner the night before the tournament began. They wanted to make it easy for Tiger to attend so he could accept the award in person.

On Tuesday of that week, Tiger played a practice round, then returned to his hotel room and declared himself too exhausted to play in the tournament. He would still have three more weeks to make the $30,000 he needed to ensure himself an exempt spot, and he was confident he could make that—and more. So he decided to withdraw and go home.

Withdrawing from a tournament that has given you a sponsor's exemption is not considered good form on the PGA Tour unless you are injured or have a serious family crisis to attend to. Being tired is not generally considered a good enough reason. But Woods probably could have gotten away with a minimal amount of criticism—after all, the tournament had given him the exemption not so much as an act of generosity but because it knew he would sell tickets—if not for the Haskins Dinner. If Tiger had withdrawn but stuck around for the dinner, the fallout would have been minor.

But that wasn't what he did. Instead, he withdrew, got on a plane, and went home, leaving the Haskins people with two hundred guests coming to honor someone who wasn't there to be honored. Maybe—*maybe*—he was too exhausted to drag himself around a golf course. But too exhausted to sit through a dinner? That wasn't going to wash.

Of course, Team Tiger—led by Norton— vehemently defended Tiger's exit. A week later, after Tiger had been roundly ripped for leaving,

Norton was still trying to claim that Tiger's behavior was just fine. "If I had it all to do over again, I'd still advise him to go ahead and leave," he claimed.

Which proves that Hughes Norton either isn't very smart or thinks the world isn't very smart (more likely the latter). This was the first glaring example of the adults letting the kid down. Someone in the group that was making itself rich off Woods—Norton, Earl Woods, Phil Knight, Fluff Cowan, *anyone*—should have sat him down and said, "Look, Tiger, maybe you can get away with blowing off the tournament. They'll still go ahead and hold it without you. But the dinner is different. That they can't hold without you. They scheduled it here and now just for you. You *must* go."

No one did that, though. Tiger took the hit— and he deserved to take it. But his flunkies let him down big-time. Weeks later Tiger publicly apologized for leaving, and the dinner was rescheduled. Months later he would admit that Dinnergate was "my one bad mistake." And Hughes Norton? "You know, I'm not sure [Tiger] would have won the next week in Vegas if he had stayed."

Sure, Hughes. You stick to that story.

O F COURSE, WOODS did go on to win the Las
Vegas Invitational the following week, which
not only made him exempt for 1997—first prize was
$297,000, which put $170,000 way back in the
rearview mirror—but also for 1998, since a win on
the PGA Tour comes with a two-year exemption.

More than that, the victory began to take the
story of Tiger to near-mythic proportions. When
he finished third in Texas the next week, then won
again at the Walt Disney/Oldsmobile Classic a
week after that, the myth makers didn't really need
hyperbole. It was during that week at Disney that
Paul Goydos, one of the wiser and more acerbic

players on the Tour, raised the oft-asked question: "Who is the best player on tour who hasn't yet won a major?" His answer was Tiger Woods. At that moment Woods hadn't yet *played* in a major as a pro, which was exactly the point Goydos was making. Woods wasn't yet twenty-one and, according to Goydos, "anyone who doesn't think he's the best player in the world right now is kidding himself."

Tiger's game left everyone gasping. He wasn't just amazingly long, he was straight as well. Whenever he needed to make a putt, he made it. When the pressure was on, he seemed to play better. A couple of stubborn naysayers couldn't help but point out that his two victories had come on easy resort courses, set up with little rough because both tournaments let amateurs play until Sunday. That meant Tiger could take out the driver and let fly without worrying about finding serious trouble if he missed a fairway. Augusta, everyone noted, seemed built for him—wide fairways, little rough. But the golf courses where the other three majors were played might be a different story. Thus far, though, Woods had blown away every challenge—

and challenger—in his path. Some had wondered if he could make $170,000 in eight weeks. He had made $723,000 in *seven*—and won twice.

Still, watching him in action off the course was discomfiting, especially to people—such as me—who had seen other gifted young athletes lose perspective because there were so many people around them constantly telling them how great they were. When Tiger spoke to the media, it was clearly a struggle for him not to roll his eyes as he answered questions. He began a lot of his answers by saying, "You guys don't understand. . . ." Actually, a lot of us did.

We knew that the Tiger being created by his image makers at IMG, Nike, and Titleist was a lot different from the Tiger who signed autographs only once in a while, who rarely spoke to his amateur playing partners or even to the little kids carrying the traveling scoreboards around the golf course. We knew that Tiger turned on the thousand-watt smile whenever a TV camera was around but could be short and surly with those he didn't deem important.

After his victory at Disney he and his handlers

tried unilaterally to close the locker room to the media. Only when a PGA Tour official intervened was the locker room reopened. "The locker room has been open on this tour for Palmer, for Nicklaus, for Watson, and everyone else," the official told Fluff, who was helping the security types guard the door. "It's open for this kid too. He's not the fifth Beatle."

Of course he wasn't. Earl and Norton never would have agreed to share billing.

THE NEW YEAR began for Tiger pretty much
the way the old year had ended. He won the
first event of 1997, the Mercedes Championships
at the La Costa Resort and Spa, beating Tom
Lehman in a playoff that was created when the last
round was wiped out by rain. Lehman hit his
tee shot into the water at the par-three playoff
hole, opening the door for Tiger. Instead of
hitting a routine shot safely to the middle of the
green, Woods stuffed a 7-iron within six inches of
the hole.

And so the legend grew.

The legend also ran into some more problems

away from the golf course. Early in the year it seemed as if every magazine in America, with the possible exception of *The Atlantic,* wanted to do a Tiger cover. GQ was no exception. Norton and the IMG gang decided this was one interview Tiger should give, reaching out to GQ's upscale readership. But they failed to do their homework. The piece was assigned to a writer named Charlie Pierce, who is no puff artist. He has strong opinions, can write like a house afire, and can cut a subject to ribbons when he wants to. Like a lot of people, Pierce had been amazed and outraged by the tone of the Gary Smith piece in *Sports Illustrated,* and he arrived for his meeting with Tiger in California looking to debunk what he and most of the planet knew was a myth: the notion of Tiger as messiah.

Tiger proceeded to make it easy for him, playing the role of a normal twenty-one-year-old. During a photo shoot, apparently trying to show off for a couple of models, he told several crude jokes, one of them a particularly tasteless gay-bashing joke. It was the sort of stuff being told around fraternity houses all over the country that week. Only, Tiger wasn't in a fraternity house at Stanford. He was in the presence of a smart, tough magazine writer who proceeded to use the jokes as the foundation for a piece that basically said, "Great golfer, yes; anything beyond that, get real."

When the piece came out in mid-March, Tiger was playing in the Bay Hill Invitational in Orlando, Florida. The smart thing to do would have been simply to say, "Mea culpa, yes, I tell dirty jokes." How many twenty-one-year-olds *don't* tell dirty jokes? It's not a crime. Instead, IMG put out a smarmy little statement over Tiger's name that said, in essence, the lesson he had learned in all this was never to trust the media. Of course. No doubt Pierce had told Tiger the jokes or forced him to tell them. Actually, Team Tiger had an even funnier theory than that: The limo driver had been wired. Otherwise Pierce never would have known that Tiger had told the jokes.

Yes, people do actually get paid money to think these things up.

AFTER LA COSTA, WOODS didn't win again before the Masters, but he played very solidly,
contending almost every week. He also took a side
trip in February to Thailand and Australia, picking
up about a million bucks in appearance money for
two tournaments. It was that trip that brought to
a head the simmering feud between Team Tiger
and me.

I had gotten off to a bad start with the Woods
family during Tiger's debut week, when *Newsweek*
had asked me to write a piece on Tiger's impact
and what it might mean to the world of golf. My
piece probably wasn't much different from all the

others on Tiger's arrival. It talked about what he could mean to the sport, his enormous potential, and the questions about just how good he might be and how soon. The trouble began—as they like to say on TV—when I drew parallels between Earl Woods and Stefano Capriati: the notion of a man building his life around his child's becoming a star, the fact that neither man had worked for a number of years prior to the child's making them rich, and the Earl/IMG relationship.

A week later another reporter came up to me at a golf tournament and said, "Earl Woods is furious that you compared him to Stefano Capriati."

"I don't blame him," I answered. "I'd be furious if someone compared me to Stefano Capriati, too—even if it were true."

Another reporter, one of a small group who had been close to the Woods family for almost as long as Norton, told me that Tiger had "gone ballistic" when he read what I had to say about his dad. Again, I didn't blame Tiger for feeling that way. A good son should always side with his dad. A couple of months later, when *Newsweek* wanted to do a cover story on Tiger's remarkable beginnings on tour, Team Tiger made the editors practically crawl as punishment for what I had written. No doubt the editors pointed out that I wasn't on staff and would probably never be allowed to darken their pages again. *Newsweek* got its cover; the Woodses got to vent.

Things got worse after that. I wrote a column in *Golf Magazine* describing Tiger's attempted locker-room closing at Disney. In the same piece I also mentioned that Peter Jacobsen had been hurt and disappointed that Tiger never got around to asking him if he minded that Fluff was leaving him—after eighteen years—to caddy for Tiger. Jacobsen would never have attempted to stand in Fluff's way, but he (and other players) thought Tiger should have had the courtesy to *ask*, anyway. It was after that column that Hughes Norton began calling my editors at *Golf Magazine*, wanting to know who my sources were and why I was being allowed to write these terrible things about Tiger. They weren't interested in the notion that I *wasn't* writing terrible things about Tiger. I was covering Tiger—I just wasn't trying to be his best friend.

Then came Tiger's trip to Thailand and Australia. I am something of a zealot on the subject of athletes running themselves into the ground chasing money. I saw it happen to Jennifer Capriati and numerous others in tennis. I've seen it happen to Greg Norman, Nick Price, Fred Couples, and Curtis Strange—to name a few—in golf. They have some success, and the offers pour in from around the world. The money is big, *unbelievably* big in some cases, and difficult to resist. But for someone who is going to be a champion for a long time, resisting it is vitally important. No matter how you go, even if it's first class or on your own plane, travel is exhausting. And when you are overseas playing for appearance fees, there are always obligations that go beyond just playing.

The way an overseas appearance by a big-name golfer works is this: Knowing that a player isn't going to traipse to Japan or Australia or Europe or Africa for mere prize money, a tournament sponsor offers him money up front. Most stars won't set foot on an airplane for less than $100,000, and the megastars usually get at least $250,000 to go anyplace. For Woods, the bidding usually begins at $400,000 and can go higher. Appearance money is verboten on the PGA Tour, and those rules are almost always enforced. That's why players are willing to travel long distances for guaranteed money.

In return for this kind of money, the sponsor expects more than just four rounds of golf. The player will normally be expected to play in a pro-am the day before the event, show up at a couple of cocktail parties or dinners to glad-hand with the sponsor's business partners or pals, and perhaps give a clinic. There are usually appearances for his own sponsors—shoe company, apparel, and so forth—worked into the week. In short, one such week is exhausting. Anything more leaves players in a state of collapse.

If you are someone like Mark Brooks or Corey Pavin or Lee Janzen and you have just won your first major title, the temptation to cash in may be overwhelming. After all, there's no guarantee that the kind of money being tossed at you will ever come your way again.

One of the first golfers to cash in on sudden stardom had been a player named Bill Rogers. He won the British Open in 1981 in the midst of a career year during which he won four tournaments. IMG put him in events all over the world during the next couple of years. He collected appearance fees everyplace he went. And Rogers never won another tournament. He was out of the game completely within five years of his huge success. His agent: Hughes Norton.

In an ideal world, agents would sift through offers and explain to a rich and famous client why most of them should be turned down: "Focus on winning major championships and you'll have all the money you could possibly need or want." But agents are bottom-line guys. They can't collect a commission on zero. This is especially true at IMG, which has its tentacles all over the world. IMG also runs tournaments and is in the business of making sure those tournaments get as many of the best players as possible. One of the ways it sells itself to young players is by promising to get them into events around the world. IMG is so good and so aggressive about sending players overseas that there is a phrase players use, "getting IMG'd," to describe those who play overseas so often that they burn themselves right out of the stardom they are seeking. No one was a better example of being IMG'd than Bill Rogers.

The last thing in the world Tiger Woods needed was to be IMG'd. To begin with, he didn't need extra money; he already had millions from his endorsement deals. There was no reason for him to play overseas except just before (as a warm-up) and during the British Open, and perhaps during golf's off-season in November and December if he wanted to take a working vacation. But there he was in February going to Thailand and Australia. The given reason for the trip to Thailand was that his mother, who is from Thailand, wanted to see her son play in her native country. Even if you accept that story, why the trip to Australia? It isn't as if Australia is a forty-five-minute hop from Thailand.

To me, the trip was a clear sign that IMG had every intention of milking Tiger for every penny it could. When I made that point on an ESPN television show called *The Sports Reporters* and referred to IMG as "IMGreedy," Norton was on the phone the next morning with George Peper, the editor of

Golf Magazine. Why Peper would get a call about something I had said on TV, I wasn't sure. In any event, Norton told Peper that I was "out to get him" and demanded a face-to-face meeting with me at the Masters.

I was amused when Norton's comments were passed on to me. At the time I barely knew the agent. I think I had met him twice and spoken to him on the phone once. One of the nice things about covering golf is that—unlike in tennis—you rarely have to deal with agents. If you want to talk to most players, you just go find them. In tennis, where access to the players is virtually nonexistent at tournaments, you are forced to go through agents. That's one of the reasons why golf's image with the public and the media is so much better than tennis's: The players actually interact with the media on a regular basis. If Norton wanted a meeting, I told Peper, I'd happily meet with him. I'm a big believer in letting people vent.

The meeting at Augusta was over breakfast. IMG was represented by Norton, the company's PR guy, Bev Norwood, and someone named Clark Jones. *Golf Magazine* was represented by

Peper, myself, and Mike Purkey, who has the dubious honor of editing my columns. For a while Norton sparred, wanting to know who my sources were on various things I had written. He kept getting angrier and angrier. Finally he said, "And I suppose you think you're funny with that 'IMGreedy' stuff! You probably heard that from someone who is out to get us!"

"Very possible, Hughes," I answered, "since I first heard it from Pete Sampras—one of your clients."

Soon Norton came to the real point of the meeting. Tiger, he explained, had a very important decision to make in the next few weeks: which golf magazine he was going to lend his name to (at a considerable price) as a "playing editor." I exploded. I knew that Peper had been working very hard to try to win Tiger away from *Golf Digest*, the other major monthly golf magazine. Clearly, Norton was threatening poor Peper by insinuating that if I didn't start behaving, he would take Tiger to *Golf Digest*. I told Norton that I didn't give a damn who Tiger "wrote" for, and that if Peper started editing what I wrote to make Team Tiger happy,

I'd quit. To Peper's credit, throughout the months when he was trying to woo Norton he had never asked me to back off from what I was reporting. He did try to mediate a truce between Norton and myself, which was both a thankless task and a futile one.

Four days later Tiger won the Masters by twelve shots and owned the golf world, the sports world, and most of the free world. Like everyone else, I was awed by his performance. What's more, he handled the press conference after his victory with remarkable grace, making sure to mention trailblazers such as Ted Rhodes, Charlie Sifford, and Lee Elder—who had flown in on Sunday to witness the historic moment. It was a great story, one I was glad to write.

A week later the Family Woods signed with *Golf Digest.* Oh, darn.

I HONESTLY THOUGHT that Tiger's victory at the Masters might put to rest the ongoing hostility between myself and Team Tiger. After all, I had written and spoken in glowing terms about his performance at Augusta—for the simple reason that there was nothing *not* to be glowing about.

And then all hell broke loose.

One incident wasn't Tiger's fault. The other one was—with, of course, some help from his friends.

Tiger's Masters victory happened to take place two days before the fiftieth anniversary of Jackie

Robinson's historic debut with the Brooklyn Dodgers. A major celebration had been planned in New York for that night. The Dodgers would be in town to play the Mets, the team that had replaced the Dodgers and Giants in New York after those two National League teams fled to the West Coast in 1958. President Clinton was scheduled to take part in the ceremony, as was Rachel Robinson, Jackie Robinson's widow.

Someone—either in the baseball hierarchy or in the White House—decided that Tiger's presence, given his breakthrough for minorities at Augusta, would add to the ceremony. Calls went out to Tiger through IMG. Tiger was traveling that day, making paid appearances in Hilton Head, South Carolina, and Atlantic City, New Jersey, as part of a deal he had with All-Star Cafes, the chain of sports bars that has signed up a bunch of big-name jocks (Shaquille O'Neal, Wayne Gretzky, Monica Seles, Andre Agassi) as front people. The plan was to send a plane to Atlantic City to bring Tiger to New York. If he wanted, he could make an appearance with the president the next day at a school and then go to Shea Stadium for the ceremony. If he only wanted to take part in the ceremony at the ballpark, that was fine, too.

Tiger said no.

According to Norton, attending the ceremony would have meant postponing—by twenty-four hours—a vacation he had planned in Mexico with some friends. Tiger just couldn't do that. I called Norton that day and asked one question: "What did you tell Tiger to do about this?"

"I didn't tell him anything," he answered. "I just laid out the pros and cons for him."

I couldn't resist. "Hughes, exactly what were the cons?"

He launched into the explanation about the vacation and his buddies. That was it. "Hughes, forget what *I* think about this," I told him. "If that's all you've got, Tiger's going to get hammered."

And, of course, he did. It didn't really matter whether you liked or disliked Bill Clinton; this was a historic occasion. Even if, as was reported by some people, Earl, the former Green Beret, didn't approve of Clinton because of his lack of a military record, what about Rachel Robinson? What about the legend of Jackie Robinson? Forty-eight hours after handling himself so magnificently at Augusta, talking about the golfers who had blazed the trail for him, Tiger had blown off the memory of the man who had blazed more trails than anyone. A friend of mine summed it up best. "It's Clinton's fault," he said. "He forgot to offer Tiger and IMG an appearance fee."

Three weeks later, when Tiger returned to the Tour, he and his band of merry men had come up with a new explanation for the blow-off. "Why didn't the president invite me *before* the Masters?" Tiger asked. "I win, then all of a sudden the day before this ceremony, he invites me at the last minute."

Well, yes, it had certainly been a last-minute invitation. But it came in response to what Tiger had done at Augusta, making history by *winning*. He didn't make history by participating; Elder had done that twenty-two years earlier. Tiger wasn't even the only minority player in the field. David Berganio, a Mexican-American who had grown

up in the L.A. barrio under far more difficult circumstances than Tiger, also played. But Berganio
didn't win. Tiger did. *That's* why he was invited.

Even as the dust was clearing from the presidential diss, another controversy broke out. This
time Tiger was little more than an innocent by-
stander. On the last day of the Masters, with Tiger
cruising to victory, Fuzzy Zoeller, the 1979 Masters champion, had been asked by a camera crew
from CNN about Tiger's performance. Zoeller is
one of the Tour's funnymen, someone who loves a
good quip and isn't above telling locker-room
jokes that would definitely be considered politi-
cally incorrect. With the camera rolling, Zoeller
brain-locked for a moment, somehow thinking he
was among friends.

"The little boy's playing great out there," he
said. Then he added, "Just tell him not to serve fried
chicken at the [Champions] dinner next year." And
then, just for good measure, as he started to walk
away, Zoeller turned back to the camera and said,
"Or collard greens or whatever it is they serve."

Zoeller might have gotten away with the little-
boy line because of Tiger's age. He might even

have gotten off with a societal slap on the wrist for bringing up the fried-chicken-and-collard-greens stereotype (he was referring to the fact that the defending champion chooses the menu each year at the Masters Champions Dinner). But the last line nailed him: "whatever it is *they* serve." There was no way to escape that line. It sounded awful, especially to an audience that didn't know Fuzzy Zoeller or care who Fuzzy Zoeller was. Zoeller and friends could have cited Zoeller's laudable record on race relations for the next hundred years and it wouldn't have mattered.

At that moment, Tiger Woods was the best-known and most-talked-about racial minority on the planet. (Tiger likes to call himself a "Cablinasian," since he is part African-American, part Thai, part Caucasian, and part Native American.) Zoeller's comments, which aired on a CNN golf show a week after the Masters, created an uproar comparable to the one set off when Los Angeles Dodgers general manager Al Campanis made the infamous comment on *Nightline* in 1987 about blacks "lacking the necessities" to manage major-league baseball teams.

Zoeller apologized. That wasn't good enough. Kmart, his longtime sponsor, dumped him from a deal worth about $1 million a year. That still wasn't enough. Zoeller, in tears, withdrew from the Greater Greensboro Open, one of his favorite events on tour, because there were threats of pickets at the event. He apologized again and said he hoped Tiger would call him on the cell phone he was keeping with him at all times so he could apologize to him personally.

Tiger was in Portland that day, with Norton, in a meeting with Nike's Phil Knight. When Zoeller's apology and phone number were delivered to him, Knight reportedly commented, "That can wait."

So Zoeller waited. Things were getting so ugly that a number of players who were also represented by IMG called the company to plead with their own agents to convince Norton that Tiger had to issue a statement of some kind. "Let Tiger say he was outraged by the comments," Steve Elkington, an IMG client, said. "But get him to say *something*."

Brad Faxon went a step further, calling Mark McCormack, the founder and chairman of the board of IMG. "Mark, Tiger has to say something," Faxon said.

"We're going to wait until they're face-to-face at a tournament," McCormack said.

"Not good enough," Faxon said. "He needs to say something right now. This is an explosive situation."

Three days after Zoeller's second apology and his withdrawal from Greensboro, Tiger did issue a statement saying he accepted the apology. In the eyes of many players, that was too late. Virtually all of them were convinced that if Zoeller had been an IMG client, a statement would have been forthcoming sooner, especially if the company felt it could save the Kmart deal. But Zoeller wasn't an IMG client, so he twisted in the wind. He did finally meet with Tiger a couple of weeks later, but little was resolved. At the U.S. Open, John Daly, a pal of Zoeller's, tried to get Tiger to play a practice round with him and Zoeller.

Tiger said no.

A LOT OF PLAYERS were going to be resentful of Tiger no matter what he did. Even though his presence was going to make all of them wealthier, there was a natural resentment toward someone who had so much so young. But there was also a small cadre of players who went out of their way to reach out to Tiger, to try to make him feel accepted as one of the guys—even though circumstances would make that virtually impossible.

One of those players was Billy Andrade. Outgoing by nature, Andrade remembered his early days on tour. "It can be very tough and very lonely for anyone," he said. "I never forgot the fact that a number of guys made a point of taking me under their wing from the beginning. I've tried to do that whenever I can with other young players."

On the day that Tiger held his "Hello, world" press conference in Milwaukee, Andrade saw him on the range warming up. He wondered if anyone had asked him about playing a practice round. "Hey, Tiger," he said casually, "got a game?"

As it turned out, Tiger didn't. So he played with Andrade's group that day. The two remained friendly through the months that followed. Tiger's best friend on tour was Mark O'Meara, who was his neighbor at Isleworth, the Arnold Palmer–owned development for the very rich outside Orlando. O'Meara and Woods often played practice rounds there when both were at home, and O'Meara became something of a big brother figure to Tiger. Others who went out of their way to befriend Tiger were Davis Love III, Faxon, and John Cook, O'Meara's best friend. Arnold Palmer and Jack Nicklaus tried to whisper in Tiger's ear whenever they had a chance, knowing how important he was to the future of their game.

Tiger took three weeks off after the Masters

and returned to play in the Byron Nelson Classic in Dallas. He arrived to find his locker stuffed with things left for him by fellow pros to sign. Most players on tour are involved with at least one charity golf event during the year, and something with Tiger's autograph on it would obviously be worth a lot of money as an auction item. Traditionally, players sign things for each other's charities and, when schedules allow, often play in them.

Billy Andrade arrived in Dallas with one thing for Tiger to sign: a golf ball. He and Faxon have run a charity event for several summers now in Rhode Island; it raises money for children at risk. One of their auction items each year is a box of golf balls, each one signed by a Masters champion. Naturally, Andrade and Faxon wanted to add a Tiger-signed ball to the 1997 collection.

Andrade walked up to Tiger in the locker room and asked him if he could take a minute to sign a golf ball for him. He was carrying a Sharpie, the special marking pen most pros carry with them for signing autographs. Tiger shook his head. "I don't sign golf balls," he said.

More and more, golf pros are refusing to sign

golf balls these days because they know that many of them aren't for legitimate autograph seekers but for collectors who sell them at a large profit. Andrade knew that. But this was different. "Tiger, this is for charity," he said, and launched into an explanation of the golf ball collection.

Tiger shook his head again. "I told you," he said, "I don't sign golf balls."

Andrade wasn't about to beg a fellow golf pro for an autograph. But he tried one more time, explaining to Woods that he could tell him exactly where this ball would end up and what it would be used for. Woods got angry. "Didn't you hear me?" he said. "I don't sign golf balls."

Andrade was furious. He had never been treated in such a manner by another pro. Jack Nicklaus had signed a ball for the collection, as had Arnold Palmer, Nick Faldo, and Tom Watson. When he told other players what had happened, they were stunned. Naturally, the story got into the media. That was bad news for Woods but good news, as it turned out, for Andrade and Faxon. Two youngsters in Rhode Island who had gotten golf balls signed by Tiger when he was still an amateur read the story. They contacted Andrade and Faxon and offered one of their balls for the collection.

Andrade and Faxon responded by inviting them to the tournament and the dinner. There actor Joe Pesci, a friend of Andrade's, bid $50,000 for the collection and then returned the Tiger ball to the two kids. The publicity surrounding the incident pushed the bidding up for the entire auction (Tiger eventually signed a lithograph to be sold for this charity event) and, according to the estimates of Faxon and Andrade, probably made the charity an extra $100,000 beyond what they would have made if Tiger had simply signed the ball.

"He did us a huge favor," Faxon said, laughing, several months later.

Tiger didn't do himself any favors, though. The incident further sullied his image. At the British Open he walked up to Faxon on the putting green just before the start of the first round and said, "You know, if you guys want me to sign a golf ball, I'll sign one for you."

This was two months after Dallas, two weeks after the auction. "Tiger," Faxon said, "thanks. But we really don't need one now."

THROUGH ALL THE off-course troubles, Tiger continued to play a lot of superb golf. He won at the Byron Nelson Classic and won again in July at the Western Open. But those who had believed that the tighter golf courses the last three majors are traditionally played on would give him problems turned out to be correct.

You don't win the U.S. Open on pure power. You don't win the British Open without superb course management. You don't win the PGA Championship without discipline. In fact, you don't win any of those titles by playing, as one pundit called it, "extreme golf." Woods learned the hard way at those three majors in 1997. At both the U.S. Open and the British Open he made more birdies than anyone else in the field. But he didn't come close to winning, either (nineteenth at the U.S. Open, twenty-fourth at the British), because he kept making big numbers. At the U.S. Open—and the PGA—double bogeys hurt him. At the British Open he made two triple bogeys and a quadruple bogey.

Tiger hadn't yet learned that one of the secrets to winning major championships is making bogeys: If you get into trouble, make certain you get out of the hole with no worse than a bogey. Everyone makes bogeys in the majors; the golf courses are too hard not to make a few of them. But those who win are those who understand that sometimes bogey is a *good* score. They chip out of trouble, take their bogey, and run to the next tee. Tiger kept trying to blast his way out of trouble and often found *more* trouble as a result. Every once in a while he would make a spectacular save that would send the crowds into a frenzy—but for every roar of approval, there were about three groans of disappointment.

Tiger's play in the last three majors was best defined by a three-hole stretch during the third round of the PGA Championship. He came to the sixteenth hole one under par for the tournament, well within striking distance of Davis Love and Justin Leonard, the coleaders at that moment, who were then at five under. He promptly hooked his drive left, into the trees, leaving himself virtually no shot to the green. Somehow he carved a shot through the trees, going under one and over another, and miraculously landed the ball eight feet from the pin. From there he made birdie. Golf just doesn't get better than that. Now he was two under.

But he drove into trouble once more at the seventeenth hole. Again he tried for a spectacular play through the trees. This time, though, he didn't escape. He had to hack out a second time, and by the time he was through, he had a double-bogey 6. So much for being two under par. Then, at the eighteenth hole, he pushed his tee shot into rough so deep that the only thing to do was pop a wedge into the fairway and try to make par from there. Not Tiger. He tried to slash the ball out of the rough and onto the green and succeeded only in wrenching his back and leaving the ball woefully short. He limped off with a bogey, a sore back, and a bruised ego. The next day he shot a discouraged 75 and finished tied for twenty-ninth place—seventeen shots back of Love.

Undoubtedly Tiger learned from those mistakes. Great players always do. But what about all the off-course mistakes? Has he learned from those?

The answer appears to be a definite maybe. After the public-relations disaster at the U.S. Open, a different Tiger showed up to play the following week at the Buick Classic in Westchester. He was never in contention all week, clearly tired. But after every round he stopped and spoke to the media, usually behind the green, since he wasn't asked to go to the media room. From that point on, Tiger spoke to the media after every round he played—good, bad, or indifferent. Even in Canada in early September when he missed the first cut of his professional career, he patiently answered questions after shooting 76 on Friday.

There was a message in all this: Given the right advice, Tiger would do the right thing. Evidently, IMG had figured out during the U.S. Open that the time had come to explain to Tiger that he couldn't blow off the media whenever he felt like it. Tiger listened and learned. That was an encouraging sign.

The only bad news through the summer and fall was that he didn't appear to be the same golfer he had been during the first six months of his career. Not only was he not a factor in the majors, he was a huge disappointment in his first Ryder Cup. When most people sized up the U.S. team and the European team, they gave the edge to the Americans—in large part because of Tiger's presence. After all, he had proven himself to be a dominant player in match play, winning eighteen straight matches en route to his three U.S. Amateur titles. No one was better, or so the thinking went, than Tiger Woods in head-to-head competition.

Only it didn't work out that way. Even in the one match he was involved in that produced a U.S. victory, it was the play of O'Meara, his partner, that spurred the win. When captain Tom Kite paired him with Justin Leonard on the second day, it took some brilliant scrambling by Leonard to pull out a tie. And then, with the U.S. team desperately trying to rally on the final day during the singles matches, the player many thought they would rally around went belly-up, losing convincingly to Costantino Rocca.

To be fair, Woods wasn't the only key player to fail in Spain. Love, coming off his emotional victory at the PGA Championship, came up empty, going 0-4 in his matches. Leonard was 0-2-2, but he played a good deal better than Tiger. The golf course, narrow and difficult, was not set up to take advantage of Woods's power. And, as he had done in the last three majors, instead of adjusting, Tiger appeared to be trying to hit the ball over buildings. That wasn't going to work. All weekend he wore a strange, confused look on his face, as if to say, "How can this be happening to me?" At one point, en route to losing a better-ball match on Saturday morning, Woods and O'Meara walked down the seventeenth fairway laughing and telling jokes. They were two down at the time. Tiger then walked onto the green and, desperately needing to sink a thirty-foot eagle putt to keep the match alive, putted the ball across the green, off the green, and *into the water*.

Maybe it all would have been different if Earl had been there. Earl had made a very public pronouncement a week earlier, complaining that he had not been invited to join the team as Tiger's companion for the week. Traditionally, when the Ryder Cup team flies to Europe on the Concorde, the players are allowed to bring along their wives or girlfriends. Those companions are also included in most of the team functions and, in fact, march in with the team during the opening and closing ceremonies. Earl felt, not without some justification, that since Tiger did not have either a wife or a girlfriend to bring on the trip, he should have been allowed to invite his father.

Although that would have been unprecedented, and Earl might have felt a bit funny walking into the opening ceremonies along with ten women (Brad Faxon, who was going through a divorce, was also without a companion) dressed in identical outfits, the case could certainly be made that each player should be allowed to bring along anyone he wishes.

But Earl couldn't just leave it at that. He couldn't resist saying that he had had more to do with Tiger's success than any of the wives had to do with their husbands'. Putting aside any debate on that issue, it was a foolish, rude, insulting, obnoxious thing to say. To top it all off, Earl announced that he was "boycotting" the Ryder Cup, that he wouldn't pay his own way to the event (or, more accurately, pay his way with his son's money) and then have to walk along outside the ropes. Earl wouldn't have done much walking under any circumstances, since he had undergone open-heart surgery in the spring. And if he had, arrangements would have been made to get him inside the ropes, the same way they were made for Davis Love's mother in 1993. But Earl had been insulted. So he stayed home.

Which raises this question: Exactly whom did Earl hurt with his boycott? It's probably a fair guess that none of the wives missed him. In all likelihood, Tiger's teammates probably weren't walking around telling people, "Gee, I wish Earl were here." One person and one person only probably missed Earl in Spain: Tiger. Whether that thought ever crossed Earl's mind is difficult to say, but if it did, it certainly didn't motivate him to hop on a plane so that he could be there to support his son.

Tiger's poor play that week probably had more to do with exhaustion than anything else. Four weeks earlier he had celebrated his first anniversary as a pro. In those first twelve months he had played in twenty-five PGA Tour events, winning an extraordinary six of them. He had also been overseas several times, had taken part in a number of lucrative one-day events (including one charity event in Pittsburgh that reportedly made a $1.8 million deal to guarantee his presence there for the next three years), and had done lengthy commercial shoots for Nike, American Express, Titleist, and Rolex. Even for a twenty-one-year-old that was a huge amount of travel, a lot of wear and tear, and a ton of glad-handing and question-answering. That's without even mentioning having to deal with all the controversies that popped up—some self-inflicted, others not—and making trips to Portland to see Phil Knight and to places such as Hilton Head and Atlantic City for restaurant openings.

Tiger's mediocre play continued throughout the fall. He missed the first cut of his professional career in Canada, and then, after the Ryder Cup, he finished the official year at the two tournaments he had won in 1996, the Walt Disney Classic (tie for twenty-sixth) and the Las Vegas Invitational (tie for thirty-sixth), and at the season-ending Tour Championship in Houston (tie for twelfth in a thirty-man field).

Clearly, no one needed a rest more than Tiger Woods. But that wasn't in the cards. Instead, November would include another trip overseas to Japan for an event sponsored by (surprise!) Nike, followed by a trip to Hawaii for a four-man exhibition involving the year's four Grand Slam winners, and finally a trip to California for the mother of all worthless made-for-TV golf events, the Skins Game. Tiger needed to play in Japan and in the Skins Game about as much as he needed to win a month's supply of golf balls. If he really wanted to play a second event in November, he could have played in the World Cup of Golf, which was being held in Kiawah Island, South Carolina, less than an hour's plane ride from his home. The organizers of the World Cup were so desperate to get him to play that they were willing to bypass the team of Davis Love and Fred Couples, who had won the event four times in the past. They told Tiger that he could pick his partner if he would just come and play.

That wasn't good enough. The money was bigger overseas. Question: Did Tiger need the extra money? Unlikely. Did IMG want to squeeze every nickel it could out of the Woods franchise? Much more likely.

And so 1997 came to an end with some questions answered, others still lingering. Could Tiger be a dominant player in a sport that is almost impossible to dominate? Absolutely. Could he produce performances under pressure that would leave people with their mouths hanging open in amazement? Unquestionably; any doubt about that was laid to rest at Augusta. Was he likely to be the best player in the world for years to come? Yes. Was he capable of learning from his mistakes? Yes.

But larger questions are still unanswered, the biggest one being this: Can he burn out chasing money all over the globe while trying to cope with the pressures of being a superstar? The answer to that, unfortunately, is yes. Tiger needs to understand one thing: He is already beyond the point where he should make *any* decisions based on money. He has financially more than taken care of his parents, he has taken care of himself, and he has provided for the next several generations of his family. His only goal from now on should be to win major championships and to play well in the Ryder Cup.

The rest doesn't matter. He can win the Byron Nelson Classic a hundred times and the Western Open another hundred and it really won't matter. What matters is how many major titles he wins. Everyone who follows golf knows that Jack Nicklaus won eighteen professional majors (and two U.S. Amateurs). Almost no one remembers that he won a total of seventy PGA Tour events. No one knows that Greg Norman has won seventy-five tournaments around the world. Everyone knows he has won only two majors and that he blew a six-stroke lead in the final round of the 1996 Masters. Tiger Woods should have one goal as a golfer: Jack Nicklaus's record in the major championships.

Obviously, he's capable of challenging Nicklaus's seemingly untouchable numbers. Just as obviously, he's going to have to improve to get there. Yes, he can dominate at Augusta, and he may very well fulfill Nicklaus's seemingly hyperbolic prediction of 1996 that Woods would win more Masters than Nicklaus and Arnold Palmer won combined—ten. But to be truly great, a player has to win on all kinds of courses under all sorts of conditions. Only four players in the history of the game have won all four majors—Nicklaus, Gene Sarazen, Ben Hogan, and Gary Player.

Tiger will join that group *if* he doesn't retire by the time he's thirty. Unfortunately, that's not an unrealistic scenario. It's easy to imagine him becoming sick and tired of the life he has been leading. If he's going to become the next Nicklaus, he has to learn to say no, most notably to IMG, which will continue to put big-money deals and lucrative guarantees on the table for him. A million bucks to go to Asia? *No!* Two million to play three exhibitions in Pittsburgh or Portland or Peoria? *No!* How about ten million for one more corporate deal? *No!* He should choose a cause that he truly cares about, start his own charity event in Orlando, and then send autographed golf balls (yes, golf balls) and lithographs to all the other charity events he's invited to.

He doesn't have to be the messiah. Let Earl propagate that fantasy, although the less Earl talks publicly, the better off Tiger will be. At one point in the summer of 1997, when he was being badgered about the fact that his swing teacher, Butch Harmon, was employed by a golf club in Houston that banned women (he has since left there), Tiger shook his head and said, "I'm just a golfer. I can't take on all causes."

There's nothing wrong with being *just* a golfer. And there's nothing wrong with picking your causes. Thus far, though, Tiger's main causes have been IMG, Nike, American Express, Titleist, and Rolex. He may want to rethink his priorities in the years to come. He certainly shouldn't try to be the most important human of the twentieth century. He isn't. And he isn't going to be the most important human of the twenty-first century, either. The corporations keep trying to create an image for him that is both false and silly. He's a bright young man who can do a lot of good for a lot of people by working very hard at his golf, by lending his name to causes that don't pay him millions up front, and by doing the right things. Like signing golf balls for charity. Like signing autographs for little kids and continuing to put on junior clinics. Like losing his entourage.

Tiger Woods can be one of the most important athletes in history. He can leave a huge imprint on his sport and his world. But he isn't going to do it by making commercials and paid appearances around the world. Does anyone remember Arthur Ashe endorsing a product? Bill Bradley? Tiger needs to work at his golf, not his portfolio. He's going to make his mark if and when he finds people who will tell him what is right rather than what will simply make him richer.

In that first Nike commercial Tiger looked into the camera and asked the world the question,

"Are you ready for me?" The answer now is an emphatic yes.

The most important question that remains unanswered, though, is this: Who is Tiger Woods? He's not the messiah, that's for certain. But, if he so chooses, he can be more than just another athlete constantly cashing in on his ability and his fame. He can be much more.

I would like to think that Tiger will make that choice. I am not yet convinced that he will.

ABOUT THE AUTHOR

A 1977 graduate of Duke University, JOHN FEINSTEIN grew up in New York City. He spent eleven years on the staff at the *Washington Post,* as well as writing for *Sports Illustrated* and *The National Sports Daily.* He also writes for *Golf Magazine, Tennis Magazine, Inside Sports,* and *Basketball America.* He is a commentator on NPR's *Morning Edition,* a regular on ESPN's *The Sports Reporters,* and a visiting professor of journalism at Duke.

His first book, *A Season on the Brink,* is the bestselling sports book of all time. *A Good Walk Spoiled* was a #1 *New York Times* bestseller in hardcover and in paperback. His other books on the subject of sports include *A Season Inside, Forever's Team, Hard Courts, Play Ball, A Civil War: Army vs. Navy,* and, most recently, *A March to Madness: The View from the Floor in the Atlantic Coast Conference.*

A Note on The Library of Contemporary Thought

This exciting new monthly series tackles today's most provocative, fascinating, and relevant issues, giving top opinion makers a forum to explore topics that matter urgently to themselves and their readers. Some will be think pieces. Some will be research oriented. Some will be journalistic in nature. The form is wide open, but the aim is the same: to say things that need saying.

Now available from

THE LIBRARY OF CONTEMPORARY THOUGHT

VINCENT BUGLIOSI

NO ISLAND OF SANITY
Paula Jones v. Bill Clinton
The Supreme Court on Trial

Coming from

THE LIBRARY OF CONTEMPORARY THOUGHT

*America's most original writers
give you a piece of their minds*

Edwin Schlossberg

Pete Hamill

Seymour Hersh

Carl Hiaasen

Anna Quindlen

William Sterling and Stephen Waite

Jimmy Carter

Robert Hughes

Susan Isaacs

Nora Ephron

Joe Klein

Donna Tartt

Don Imus